SOCIOLOGY:

A STUDY OF SOCIETY'S GREAT UNDERLYING CONSCIOUSNESS

RESEARCH AND APPLICATIONS

JONNY BELL

WHY YOU SHOULD READ THIS BOOK

This book will help you understand the great science of sociology. Sociology reaches beyond the natural world of biology and chemistry to something much more subtle, more nuanced: the very science of human interaction. This book features sociology's vast history: from the very first questions of human interaction to the civil right's revolts of the past century. It lends you an in-depth understanding of the most important sociological studies of human behavior; the results often reveal something lurking, something a little "off." It forces you to question whether or not you're in control of your mind and your actions. How much can you know yourself without the outside influence of your greater society? How much do outsiders—people you don't even know on the street—alter your everyday actions? It further explains the ways in which sociologists create theories about people and asks questions about the future of modern sociology. How far will this scientific study take society, and will it have the ability to rectify all inequality, all unfairness? Feminists, civil rights activists, and people around the world rely on the research and findings of sociological evidence to open their eyes to the truth lurking beneath the surface of their society. Allow yourself access to the truth as well.

Table of Contents

CHAPTER 1. WHAT IS SOCIOLOGY?

Sociology studies human social behavior: the way humans exist in a greater society and alongside other individuals. It studies the origins of this social behavior, its development over time, and its various organizations and institutions in the modern sphere. The science utilizes empirical investigation and critical analysis in order to create a broad realm of research. Its attempt is to reach toward a greater realization of humanity.

Sociology's traditional focus falls in law, sexuality, religion, social mobility, and social stratification.

HISTORY AND BACKGROUND OF SOCIOLOGY

The history of Sociology dates back several thousand years. A human's natural instinct is to ask questions, to feel innate curiosity; therefore, the human of several thousand years ago popped the first question: why do people live and associate the way they do?

The original broad questions are associated with Greek philosopher Plato; the first specific research is found as far back as 1086. 1086 brought the Domesday Book: a research-driven analysis of the greater countryside of England and Wales. William the Conqueror ordered this research to discover how much each man had in terms of land and cattle. Although the research took form in order to uncover how many taxes were due, this produced the first real study of specific people in relation to their neighbors and countrymen. From the study, William the Conqueror could digest the unique social structure in a town: who was rich and who was poor. Furthermore, ancient philosopher Confucius wrote much about various social roles and their importance in keeping society afloat. There is further evidence of sociological research in ancient Israel, allowing modern sociologists to understand that they are not alone in their endeavors.

IBN KHALDUN: THE FIRST FATHER OF SOCIOLOGY

The oft-thought premier sociologist is Ibn Khaldun: a 14th century North African Arab Islamic scholar. In 1377, Khaldun wrote the Muqaddimah, an early view of the world's history. Modern scholars proclaim this work as the first analysis of the philosophy of history and sociology. It further parses through Islamic political theory and natural sciences like biology and chemistry.

In the Muqaddimah, Khaldun brings understanding to the past historical records. He says that all past works tended toward opinion, were over-confident in their sources, and had an intrinsic desire to praise the rulers at the time in order to gain fame and favor. He also says that past works ignored the laws governing and transforming human society. His analysis of human society begins with a topic called Asabiyyah. In Arabic, this means clanism, communitarism, or nationalism. He utilizes this term to describe the cohesion in a greater human community, the link that bonds between humans living all together. He says that the bond forms in every level of society: from the very poor levels to the very high levels. However, he maintains that this bond is the strongest in groups of nomads and depletes in higher societies. He analyzes the ways in which monarchies rise and fall to pave the way for greater civilizations to take form.

These initial theories of cohesion are still utilized in modern sociology to illustrate community organization.

Ibn Khaldun further discussed the theory of social conflict. He brings this theory to light with regards to his very ingrained ideas of town vs. desert. The town has the wealth and the power whereas the desert must fight for resources. Khaldun's theory stretches throughout all societies. Social conflict is, essentially, the acts of one party against the acts of another for power or resources. Essentially, there is a constant struggle between different social parties in order to maintain their desired resources or interests. Oftentimes, the parties with the greater initial resources will conquer over the parties fighting for the resources. Greater resources always equates greater power. This ancient theory from Khaldun is actually the main proponent in Karl Marx's argument for socialism.

Khaldun initiates a relationship between social conflict and social cohesion. He states that parties rise to power if they have a greater social cohesion, and that this social cohesion can be intensified with religious purpose. However, he states that every cohesive party has within it, at a very basic level, the possibility to eventually fall to another cohesive party. He says that these possibilities stem from psychological, political, sociological, and economical factors.

MODERN SOCIOLOGY AND AUGUSTE COMTE

Modern sociology grew in the enlightened years after the French Revolution in the 18th century. A French man named Emmanuel Joseph Sieyes coined the term: sociologie. However, 19th century's Auguste Comte formulated the science into its current stance. He wanted to utilize scientific studies in order to unify human societal studies and thus bring a sort of balance in the social order. At the time, he thought that a person passed through several stages in his life in a sort of process. If Comte could understand that process, Comte could rectify all social problems in the world. This idea presented quite a feat. He developed his book, The Course in Positive Philosophy, in the years 1830-1842. His initial positivity principles were based on knowledge processes. He said that all knowledge begins with a theological formation. Some sort of supernatural power like a spirit or a god, said Comte, explained this initial state. Afterwards, this theological formation moved toward its metaphysical formation. In this formation, the knowledge was explained by a sort of abstract philosophy. Afterwards, the knowledge was explained and proven through experimentation and comparison. When this process occurred, Comte explained, the knowledge became positive. Therefore, according to his theory, if something is positive, it is absolute knowledge; it is completely formed in the brain and backed up by scientific understanding.

Of course, in relation to this theory, Comte was discussing knowledge processes over several hundreds of years. He spoke of tribes who had no knowledge of anything but existence in the theological stage. He spoke of peoples in the age after enlightenment who were able to understand abstract philosophies. And then he spoke of peoples in the years after the revolution: when science was a very real, tangible thing one could utilize to create positive knowledge.

KARL MARX AND CLASS THEORIES

Karl Marx is of deep interest in sociology studies. In the 19th century, he was incredibly concerned with class-consciousness. He felt that greater society was formulated through its obsession with material consumption. He felt that this drive to own materials created deep class-consciousness in every level of wealth. He noted that higher society looked down on lower society's lack of material possessions. He was disgusted with his notation that the wealthy class had power and greater material possessions; he felt that this class further controlled all means of communication and the greater government. He understood that the more powerful class would alter the economy in order to favor their own conditions. He generalized that there would be a class revolt: the lower classes against the higher classes. This again refers back to Khaldun's theories that all controlling societies contain within them the very seeds that will ultimately destroy them.

Karl Marx rejected Comte's positivity theories. Like Comte, however, he wanted to create a science of society and is therefore regarded as another father of modern sociology.

Chapter 2. Important Case Studies in Sociology

Several major sociological studies have been conducted over the years; these studies have formed and developed the greater sociology field and strengthened grasp on understanding humanity. Understand the research and the findings to learn how, exactly, sociology pinpoints the ways in which humans live in a greater society.

Study 1: The Protestant Ethic and the Spirit of Capitalism

German sociologist and economist Max Weber wrote *The Protestant Ethic and the Spirit of Capitalism* in 1904-1905. This text was a groundbreaking maneuver in the fields of economic sociology. Generally, the text displays Weber's arguments that Puritan ethics and ideas spawned capitalism. Karl Marx inspired much of his work in this text; however, Weber was not a Marxist.

Weber's initial question in the text was this: What, in the greater Western civilization, has formed a culture so dependent on universal values? The west was, at the time, the only place in the world with proper scientific knowledge—knowledge that wasn't based on old wives' tales, for example. There was an empirical knowledge in the west that was rational and systematic unlike anywhere else. Weber extended this scientific knowledge to formulate an analogy for the western world's capitalism. He said that only in the western civilizations had capitalism formed into a pursuit of an ever-renewable profit.

To answer his question, Weber found that Protestants were compelled on a religious level to work incredibly hard in their secular vocation. With this ever-working mentality, this person was bound to accumulate more money. Furthermore, these religions rejected the idea of wastefulness and luxurious lifestyles. They also rejected giving money to charity because this promoted ideas of begging. Weber said that instead of giving money to charity or spending money, people in these religions invested the money. It was, essentially, thought to be the "smart thing to do" and in accordance with god. Therefore, the more they worked, the more they invested. The more they worked via their religious doctrine, the stronger capitalism became.

STUDY 2: ASCH CONFORMITY EXPERIMENTS

Solomon Asch conducted the 1950's Asch Conformity Experiments in order to demonstrate the power of conformity in society. He demonstrated that simple, objective facts have no match to the greater power of conformity.

Asch's study asked groups of students to participate in a vision test. Every single one of the participants except for one participant was a collaborator with Asch's study. Therefore, they were told to act in a certain way in order to see how the very last, unassuming student would react.

The participants who were "in on" the study were asked various questions about an image. The image displayed lines: A, B, and C. They were asked how long each line was, which line was longest, etc. The questions were generally easy and required common sense to answer correctly. The students were told to answer the first few questions correctly at first and then answer incorrectly afterwards. The students said their answers out loud in front of the student who didn't know how to answer. All the students were told to answer in precisely the same way.

When the student who was not "in on" the game was asked the same questions, Asch found that one-third of the time, this student answered concurrently with the wrong answers the other students gave. He found that forty percent of the time, the student gave both wrong and right answers. Only one-fourth of the time did the student act in defiance of the wrong answers and answer with obvious correct answers.

These experiments have been consistent over many age groups and different sized groups. The power of society's influence is clearly overarching.

STUDY 3: THE COMMUNIST MANIFESTO BY KARL MARX AND FRIEDRICH ENGELS

As mentioned in chapter one, Karl Marx was one of the premier fathers of modern sociology. His book, the *Communist Manifesto*, was written in 1848 and is now regarded as one of the most influential politically driven writings of all time. He discusses class struggles and society in the greater sphere of politics.

The Communist Manifesto rose out of slum working conditions in 19th century England, Germany, and France. The lower class lived in ultimate poverty and had slim political representation. The book was created with four sections. His first section relates Communists' theories and the unfortunate relationship between the upper class and the lower class. His second section discusses the relationship between the communist party and the lower class. The third section brings out the flaws in past socialist literature, and the fourth section brings understanding of the communist party in relation to other political parties.

Marx said that the communist movement rose from an objective study of history: from an understanding of class struggles and lower class exploitation. He said that capitalisms necessary next step was socialism.

STUDY 4: MILGRAM OBEDIENCE STUDIES BY STANLEY MILGRAM

Stanley Milgram conducted the Milgram Obedience studies in the years of 1960-1974. He analyzed the limitations of society pressure, and dug up some very peculiar evidence.

During his study, a sort of young and trusting subject entered a fake laboratory and was told that a learning experiment was going to occur. The subject was told to act like a teacher and present some test questions to someone acting like a student. Every time the student gave a wrong answer, the "teacher" was told to give the learner an electric shock. When the learner gave two wrong answers in a row, the electricity was increased. The electric shock machine was labeled very clearly with: small shock, medium shock, high shock, very high shock, intense shock, extra intense shock, severely dangerous shock, and XXX with 450 volts of electricity.

During the experiment, however, the "learner" did not

actually receive any of the shocks. The learner pretended to receive the shocks: he would squirm and cry out. If the "teacher" tried to protest and stop the test, the researcher had to tell him that the experiment must continue. He would continuously say: "The experiment requires that you continue."

The experiment asked the question: "Would the teachers go all the way up to the 450 volts and fake-shock the learner?" In fact, the very first experiment showed 65% of the teachers administering this 450 volts.

In additional experiments, Milgram varied conditionals. He utilized only women; he utilized "learners" who complained of heart conditions; he changed the environment. No matter what he changed in the experiment, the results were exactly the same. Nothing mattered.

Prior to the experiment, Milgram asked many sociologists, psychologists, and philosophers what they thought would ultimately occur in the experiment. Overall, they said that approximately one in one thousand people would go all the way up to 450 volts. One in one thousand versus the actual amount: 65%. Furthermore, Milgram asked people what they would do if they were faced with the same situation. Invariably, most of them said that they would not go all the way up to 450 volts.

These results are particularly terrifying. The experiment proclaims an incredible difference between what people say they'll do versus what they'll actually do. The researcher telling them they must go on is their social pressure, and it forces them to administer great, if false, physical pain to another.

STUDY 5: THE SUICIDE STUDY

Suicide had been a long unstudied realm in sociology until Emile Durkheim's book, *Suicide*, written in 1897. The book presented a case study: an example of suicidal sociological monograph.

Durkheim discussed the suicide rates across various societies. He found that less Catholics than Protestants committed suicide because of their greater social religious control. He further found that more men committed suicide than women, more single people committed suicide than married people, more childless people committed suicide than people with children, more soldiers committed suicide than non-soldiers, and more people committed suicide in peace times than war times.

Durkheim's argument was that suicide rates lay in social factors, not in a person's individual personality. He saw that suicide rates varied in various places and various times, and therefore inspected the manner in which people are integrated in these different societies. He said that suicide rates differ in alternate social contexts.

He named three types of suicide:

ANOMIC SUICIDE:

Durkheim said this occurs when disintegrating societal forces create a feeling of loneliness in the individual. Examples of anomic suicide are often teen suicides, suicides as a result of sexual abuse, or suicides as a result of alcoholic parents.

ALTRUISTIC SUICIDE:

This type of suicide occurs when there are incredible social forces that maintain excessive regulation. Examples of altruistic suicide are suicides for religious or political reasons.

EGOISTIC SUICIDE:

This type of suicide occurs when a person feels detached and separate from the rest of his society. Normally, people find homes in society via their work or their social bonds. When a person loses these ties to society, however, he is more likely to look to egoistic suicide. An example of this is when elderly people choose to commit suicide after retirement and lost friends.

STUDY 6: THE PRESENTATION OF SELF IN EVERYDAY LIFE BY ERVING GOFFMAN

The Presentation of Self in Everyday Life was written and published by Erving Goffman in 1959. In order to make his point, he utilizes theater imagery to portray person-to-person interaction in a greater society.

Goffman said that every day presents a stage on which people present themselves in various roles. He said that every social interaction has main players and audience members. He further stated that for every stage there is also a back stage; on this back stage, people can relax and actually get rid of the roles they've been playing on their life stage. He called this his dramaturgical framework.

The main concepts of this dramaturgical framework are:

Performance: This refers to an individual's actions in front of a sort of audience. Through this performance, this individual renders meaning to himself and to his situation. The performances are meant to lend an impression and confirm the individual's identity.

Setting: The setting is the place the individual chooses to act out his performance. The setting includes any scenery or props in that desired location. The individual must base his performance according to the location he's chosen.

Appearance: Goffman says that an individual's appearance translates the individual's social status. The appearance communicates status, gender, age, occupation, and personal commitments.

Manner: The individual's manner refers to the actual behavior during the performance. An individual can appear dominant, aggressive, sad, happy, etc. The manner is most apparent when it works in contradiction with the individual's appearance. For example, if the individual is very mean and aggressive but is wearing a sweet paisley dress, the audience will be incredibly put-off.

Front: The individual's "front" is the exact idea the individual would like to convey to the greater audience. He lends a certain impression with his manner and his appearance.

Front Stage, Back Stage, Off Stage: The front stage is the area of life in which an individual presents his act to an audience. Back stage is the area in which an individual can completely unwind and be himself. He no longer portrays a role. Off stage is the area in which an individual actually meets with people from the front stage audience and interacts with them. Other performances may arise from this interaction.

Study 7: The McDonaldization of Society by George Ritzer

George Ritzer's analysis creates an understanding of the ways in which McDonald's and the greater fast food industry's principles have affected American society.

According to George Ritzer, McDonaldization is "the process by which the principles of the fast-food restaurant are coming to dominate more and more sectors of American society as well as the rest of the world" (Ritzer, 1993:1). These principles have spread to other restaurants, other stores, learning, newspapers, and childcare in something called the Chain mentality.

The Five Themes of McDonaldization:

Efficiency: Efficiency, in Ritzer's writings, relates to meeting a specific, rapid end without great effort or cost. This is, at its core, for the interests of the business. However, the advertisements peg the customers. Think of: the drive-thru at your local McDonald's, self-serve gasoline, salad bars, ATM's, and self-serve soda fountains. The customer pays for the privilege to do the work himself. He must learn to operate technology and often pay high prices. As this occurs, the business operates even more efficiently and maintains a greater profit margin.

Calculability: The fast-food industry's main emphasis is on quantity over quality. Think of the Big Mac, the Big Gulp, or Wendy's Biggie Meals. All of these refer to the size of their products—not their quality. Further "quick skinny fixes" advertise that time is much more valuable than losing weight safely and reasonably.

Predictability: The fast-food industry creates environments that meet people's ready expectations. People want to be certain of their experiences before they pay for them. Therefore, they remember the fun of last week's out-of-town McDonald's experience and are ready for a similar experience at their in-town McDonald's. McDonald's—and the rest of the world—are creating structured, controlled environments so that people feel safe. That's why there are so many sequels for the big blockbuster hits.

Increased Control and the Replacement of Human Beings with Non-Human Technology: These last two processes of McDonaldization are linked. When the industry replaces a human with technology, the industry maintains greater control of its operations. These days, everything is under the control of a computer. People can individually check out at supermarkets, and airplanes can operate by themselves.

STUDY 8: THE HISTORY OF SEXUALITY BY MICHEL FOUCAULT

Michel Foucault wrote The History of Sexuality during the years of 1976 through 1984. He wanted to disprove the idea that western civilization simply did not discuss sexuality. Because the books were written during a time of the sexual revolution, many believed that sexuality had been completely forbidden.

Foucault's questions that he chose to answer throughout the books were the following:

1. Is it historic to trace sexual repression to the bourgeois rise of the 17th century?
2. Does our society express power in terms of regression?
3. Is modern sexuality discussion a break from historical repression or simply a part of the greater history?

During the book, Foucault does not contradict the fact that sex was not discussed openly throughout Western civilization. He tried to understand why humanity suddenly held a desire to learn and discuss sexuality after so many years of repression.

Foucault analyzed the bourgeois and sexual repression first. He understood that the bourgeois valued work ethic and did not waste life on frivolity or sexual endeavors. Sex was unproductive. The bourgeoisie began to control the knowledge people had about sex, thus trying to gain further power over the people.

However, Foucault knew this wasn't the entire history of sex. He looked to sexuality in ancient Greece and Rome. Sex was erotic, normal—an everyday occurrence. He traced the path from this sex normalcy to the sexual repression and back again to current, earnest discussions of sexuality.

Chapter 3. An Extensive Look at Positivism

One of the fathers of modern sociology, Auguste Comte, developed the scientific theory of positivism. He wanted to analyze the greater societal world with series of experiments and scientific research. His theory on positivism stated that positivism created information from logical and mathematical treatments. He stated that the only truth, the only knowledge a person could have was found in this scientifically researched knowledge. Because Comte could apply these theories to the physical world with things like gravity and biology, Comte proclaimed that he could administer positivism onto the societal world. He said that much like the physical world, the societal world operated with regards to scientifically proven laws.

Positivism in Comte's History

Auguste Comte originally described positivism in his book, *The Course in Positive Philosophy* in the mid 19th century. In the book, he states that people had to make sense of the physical sciences prior to applying physical science research techniques to the main monster of all the sciences: human society itself. He said it was a natural progression.

Comte prescribes three phases in society's quest for "truth" and knowledge. These phases were theological, metaphysical, and positive. The first phase, the theological, was based on belief in god or spirits. This initial phase undergoes understanding of humankind's place in the church. It does not acknowledge questions of existence, it simply believes in existence beneath god. This phase of theology occurred in the years before the Enlightenment: the years in which populations simply took their church-given facts and accepted them as truth.

The next phase, the metaphysical phase, occurred in the years following the Enlightenment. This was a time churning with rationalism. Humanity was invested, at this stage of understanding, with certain rights.

The final stage was the positive stage. During this positive stage, Comte maintained that individual rights were far more important than any specific person's ruling. Therefore, the common man's rights were greater than the king's rule. The interest or curiosity of just one person could create anything.

None of these stages can occur without the completion of the one previous. Comte understood that the past gave way for future, better realms. This idea of progress was key in the beginning schools of sociology. Find this theory again with Karl Marx, a proclaimed non-follower of Comte's theories.

POSITIVISM IN DURKHEIM'S HISTORY

Durkheim, who published the study on Suicide listed in Chapter 2, analyzed Comte's work and added his own insight, refining the methods of positivity. He maintained that social sciences were logical next-steps to physical sciences. However, Durkheim saw that the social sciences required a more specific, distinct sociological scientific methodology than regular, physical sciences. He created great establishment in practical social research: things that stretched to study political science and market research throughout the years.

SOCIETY AFFECTS THE INDIVIDUAL

A very important look at positivism is found with the aforementioned Suicide book written by Durkheim. He analyzed various society scenarios. He looked at places and periods of time and saw variances in the amounts of suicides that occurred during those times. He learned that the individual did not have complete control over his suicide; his surroundings had a greater impact on his suicide. This is a prime example of the ways in which positivism can assist scientists in understanding the greater social sphere. Sociologists can look at numbers objectively and understand the ways in which these numbers affect people's internal psyches on an individual level.

LOGICAL POSITIVISM

Logical positivism was an early 20th century idea of positivism. It subscribed to the idea that knowledge comes from both empiricism and rationalism. Empiricism is the idea that evidence one observes is indispensable to knowledge; this aligns well with the original ideas of positivism. Rationalism, on the other hand, maintains that knowledge further requires a component that one cannot readily find in observation.

The idea of logical positivism grew in the years after World War I in a group called the First Vienna Circle. The group rejected Comte's ideas of metaphysics, especially its ontology and synthetic a priori ideas. After the group broke up, many of its members moved to the United States and became major influences on American sociology. Unfortunately, in the years after 1950, the science has been regarded as dead.

CRITICAL REALISM

These days, positivism has largely turned to a science called "Critical Realism." Critical realism is a philosophical approach to describe the relationship between the natural world and the sociological world. Its approach is associated with a man named Roy Bhaskar, who states that there are two great terms that marry together to form critical realism: transcendental realism and critical naturalism.

Transcendental Realism is an attempt to create an order for scientific investigation. In order for this investigation to work, the object of the investigation must have real mechanisms with the ability to be actualized. When the mechanisms are actualized, the object must create a particular outcome. This transcendental realism is directly contrasting the ideas of empiricism. Empiricism states that scientists can simply watch cause and effect and create their theories from there. Transcendental Realism allows the scientist to create causes for desired effects in order to understand them better. Therefore, scientists can continue to fine-tune their past theories and create better concepts.

Critical naturalism takes this transcendental realism and prescribes it to both physical scenarios and sociological scenarios. However, critical naturalism maintains that the human world is very different from the physical world. Therefore, the strategies imposed upon the human world must be very different.

Chapter 4. Understanding Antipositivism

Antipositivism is a rejection of positivism. It is the belief that the natural world's scientific investigations cannot align with the investigations of the social realm. It states that sociologists must reject empiricism when they conduct their social research. The social world cannot be viewed objectively; it holds too many abstract ideas.

Antipositivist proponents utilize research methods such as ethnographic fieldwork, open-ended interviews, and conversation analysis. Positivists generally utilize experiments and statistical surveys, much like scientists who study the natural world. Positivists maintain that the social realm can be held objectively.

The Original Concept of Antipositivism

The original rejection of positivism came from Karl Marx, the writer of *The Communist Manifesto*. He lived in the years prior to formal social science; however, he held fierce denial of Comtean sociological positivism. Other 19th century intellectuals like the Hegelians questioned empirical social analysis as well, creating the groundwork for antipositivism.

Durkheim's views on positivism certainly tweaked the initial Comtean views. He stated that sociological studies required a more sociological-based experimentation process. He understood that studying social structures was the next step after studying the natural world; however, he maintained that there were underlying differences.

Other antipositivist academics like Wilhelm Dilthey theorized the great distinctions between the natural world and the social world. He and his contemporaries outlined the abstract meanings and symbolisms involved in the social realm versus the very concrete facts outlined in the natural world.

At the beginning of the 20th century, a group of German sociologists introduced the very first version of sociological antipositivism. They stated that sociological research should focus on human cultural values, norms, symbols, and social processes. Not only that, they stated that this research should be completely subjective rather than the objective ideas of positivism.

A man named Ferdinand Tonnies outlined the two most important concepts in human association: community and society. In antipositivity, one's reality cannot be understood without these concepts. Tonnies formulated two more concepts in antipositivity: the realm of conceptuality and the realities of social action. He stated that the realm of conceptuality should be treated in a deductive, non-scientific way, while the realities of social action could be treated empirically—in a scientific manner.

The break between concept and reality in antipositivity is incredibly important and, according to antipositivists, pushes it away from natural sciences into its own realm of scientific understanding.

THE INDIVIDUAL VERSUS THE GREATER

SOCIETY

Antipositivism rejects the idea that Durkheim illustrates in his suicide study. His suicide study proclaims that the individual's suicide rate is actually altered completely by the outside structure of the society. Therefore, the place or the time creates a higher or lower suicide rate. However, antipositivism would argue that suicide is a very personal, subjective thing. They would argue that each person had his own perspective on his life and his surroundings, and that suicide must be read on a person-to-person basis in order for it to be truly understood.

CHAPTER 5. STRUCTURAL FUNCTIONALISM

Structural functionalism is a theory of sociology that understands society as a complex system of working parts. Each part, according to this theory, has a purpose to promote the society's stability and solidarity. The approach undertakes a broad overview of society: a macro-level orientation. From this broad overview, the theory understands society's evolution like that of an organism's evolution. It focuses on both social structure and social functions.

Structural functionalism looks at the functions of each of society's constituent elements: customs, norms, traditions, and institutions. Herbert Spencer promoted this with an analogy. He said that each norm, custom, tradition, and institution is like an organ working through its functions in a greater body.

EMILE DURKHEIM AND STRUCTURAL FUNCTIONALISM

Positivism's friend Emile Durkheim provided much insight in the field of structural functionalism, as well. He asked the question: how do societies maintain their stability, on an internal level, and survive over long periods of time? He suggested that societies are composed of different parts, that they are segmented. These equivalent parts are joined together with common symbols or shared values—shared things like religion. He utilized the term "mechanical solidarity" to describe these "social bonds, based on common sentiments and shared moral values." His ideas related, as well, to more industrialized, modern societies. He said that although many industrialized societies promote workers who must operate on very different tasks in order to rev the engine of their greater society, these works are held together by organic solidarity or "social bonds, based on specialization and interdependence."

Structural functionalism takes all that Durkheim said about the cohesiveness in a particular society and strengthens it. It states that all members of the great society are working toward a single, great equilibrium.

CRITICISMS OF STRUCTURAL FUNCTIONALISM

Structural functionalism was a great influence in the early 20th century and reached its height in the 1940s and 50s. In the 1960s, sociologists criticized functionalism's inability to account for social change. It was also unable to accommodate structural contradictions and conflict. Furthermore, it ignored issues of race, class, and gender—all things that created conflict in a greater society. Structural functionalism accounted for orderly change through time; however, it allowed no strange and bizarre outside currents to change a society. It held no realms to study this.

Further criticism was thrown at the fathers of structural functionalism: people like Parsons, Durkheim, and Marx. Parsons wrote his theories on orderly change in the years after World War II in a society that was in complete upheaval. Generally, his writing promoted an organization of society in a time when organization and safety seemed an off-bet. His theories may have strengthened people's thoughts in their society; they may have given him and others hope. Durkheim, on the other hand, faced criticism for his affinity for guild socialism in relation to structural functionalism.

Other criticisms of structural functionalism were found in direct arguments that it is tautologous. It is tautologous in its attempt to analyze the development of social institutions only through the various events that happened to create the social institutions. Therefore, the theory explains in a sort of circle that holds no definition for future findings.

Furthermore, structural functionalism drew a sort of easy structure of society. It held no room for individual agency. Individuals, in this theory, were puppets trying to enact out the greater society's goals.

Chapter 6. Conflict Theory and an Unequal Society

Social conflict theory is a dramatic opposition to structural functionalism. Conflict theory states that a society is a great sphere of inequality that creates constant conflict. From this conflict comes social change. This perspective charges with the idea that society benefits only a few at the expense of the poor, working class. Social inequality seems, also, to link to race, class, sex, and age. A social conflict theorist will investigate a society with ideas of a dominant group versus a minority group. Does any of this sound familiar? Does Karl Marx come to mind?

Karl Marx: The Father of Conflict Theory

German philosopher, sociologist, and economist Karl Marx created many theories that honed conflict theories in the 19th century. His theory of capitalism maintained that all human beings must be productive; that is, if people want to survive, they have to work. In relation to this work idea, he maintained that people have two types of relationship to this work that must occur. People are either the owners of this productive property or people are the workers, the formers of this productive property.

This clash between the two classes, the upper and the lower class, lies at the very heart of Karl Marx theories. He looked around him at 19th century France, Germany, and England and saw poor working conditions and incredibly desperate people. He outlined social conflict: the struggle in a society for limited resources; he further studied class conflict: the ways in which this society creates its limited resources and material goods.

KARL MARX AND CLASS CONFLICT

Remember that Karl Marx lived in a time of terrible lower class working conditions, the very beginnings of industrial capitalism. His belief resided in the fact that the owners of these industries were capitalists. These people operated these industries, opened industries in search of more profit.

From this industrial capitalism, the two classes formed: the lower class, or the proletariats, and the upper class, the bourgeoisie. The proletariats sold their labor, their ability to work, in order to survive. This complete break between the two classes allowed Marx to believe that capitalism would lead to eternal class conflict.

Furthermore, Marx believed that this capitalism system would force the workers into feelings of alienation. The workers, he said, would feel isolated and miserable because they lacked power in their own lives, in their own societies. Karl Marx believed that this alienation and complete break between classes illustrated a need for an entirely new system. He stated that socialism was the only way that economic production could provide for every single member of a society without feelings of alienation or working for nothing. Quite obviously, socialism did not quite work out.

OTHER CONFLICT THEORY PROPOSITIONS

Karl Marx was not the only one with theories relating to this issue of conflict theory. As aforementioned, Weber created a theory about protestant work ethic. He stated that Protestants worked with a religious zeal in their secular work places and thus elevated capitalistic endeavors in the greater society. Furthermore, Gumplowicz stated that societies evolved out of war and conflict; conflict leads to still more at-peace conflict with slave versus master dichotomies. The Feminine Conflict theory states that women's historical oppression will force them to conflict with men and work for power and resources from the "higher power." This conflict theory can arch worldwide as well. World systems theory states countries must compete with each other for wealth and technology. Bigger, more powerful countries always take the resources of the lower countries. They utilize their greater technology in order to turn those resources into good that they can sell back to those countries they stole the resources from.

SOCIAL CONFLICT IN MODERN TIMES

Today, social conflict provides a backdrop of modern society. It understands society as a sphere of inequality that creates constant unrest and change. Today's sociologists actually utilize social conflict theories in order to study consistent conflicts between upper classes and lower classes in a society that continues to promote capitalism. This perspective allows easy recognition of the relationship between the wealthy classes and the poor classes, the white classes and the people of color classes, and men and women. Sociologists with complete acceptance of social conflict theories would argue that powerful people—the Marxist's bourgeoisie—will do anything to maintain their power and money. He would argue that lower classes will continue to struggle to eek through a rocky society.

MODERN EXAMPLE OF CONFLICT THEORY: DRUG ABUSE AND CRIME

Conflict theorists argue that modern criminal justice works for the upper classes while continually punishing the lower classes. Petty street crimes are often punished severely, while big-scale business crimes—think Enron—are all but washed away. If someone steals a television, they might have more time in jail than a person who stole millions through their shady business dealings. This provides an example of the continuation of higher classes in their quest to maintain their high position.

Conflict theory further reaches the drug abuse trend in the United States. Social class affects drug abuse rates exponentially. Drug abuse is found most readily in politically powerless neighborhoods and towns—places where income and education levels are quite low.

MODERN EXAMPLE OF CONFLICT THEORY: WEALTH AND POWER INEQUALITY

Despite the United State's purported values and assurance of equality, meritocracy, and the pursuit of the American dream, the country sure has an incredible level of social and economic inequality. In 2007, Domhoff found that 1% of the American households owned 34.6% of privately held American wealth. The next 19% of American households owned 50.5% of American wealth. Therefore, the top 20% of Americans own 85% of all the American private wealth. The other 80% must scrimp and save and work with the remaining 15% of the wealth. This illustrates the complete inequality demonstrated in conflict theory. There is a dramatic power competition between the lower and the higher class. Furthermore, lower class Americans have a lack of health care, a higher risk of drug abuse and violent crimes, and a lack of social network in order to move up in the world and find opportunities.

Chapter 7. Purport of Public Sociology

Public sociology works to push past the academic sociology spheres in order to engage with a greater, more diverse audience. Public sociology is a particular style of sociology rather than another theory or method, as outlined in the previous chapters. It finds a contrast with professional sociology—an academic sociology form concerned only with professional sociologists.

Michael Burawoy, a sociologist, promotes public sociology in order to engage with the greater public. He works to engage with the public to spawn debates, helping them to affirm greater understanding of public policy, purposes of social movements, political activism, and institutions of civil society.

Public Sociology History

Herbert Gans introduced public sociology rather recently: in his 1988 address called "Sociology in America: The Discipline and the Public." From then on, many books have been written illustrating public psychology like Riesman's *The Lonely Crowd* or Robert Bellah's *Habits of the Heart*. In 2004, Michael Burawoy became the President of the American Sociological Association and created a public sociology platform, thus charging the phrase into much sociological light.

Since its creation, public sociology has been under much

debate. Because it detracts from the academic areas of normal sociology, many have begun to question what the exact purpose of sociology is and what the purpose could become.

PUBLIC SOCIOLOGY'S PURPOSE

When Michael Burawoy was making a personal statement for his presidential election, he created a wonderful summary of the ways in which public sociology is beneficial for the greater world. He said that because sociology was meant to mirror the rest of society, sociology must inform and define the public's debate about class and racial inequalities; it must provide information about gender regimes, market fundamentalism, environmental degradation, and violence. Public sociology, according to Burawoy, pushes beyond the academic realms to greet new social movements and media audiences. Public sociology churns debates in all contexts, in all areas of society. After these debates begin, public sociology returns with theory and research in order to bring direction to each debate. As the sociologists bring understanding of sociology to the public, the public can begin to see gaps in the greater society and understand how their world can become different. Burawoy states that public sociology's aim is to turn private, academic concerns into public issues—issues that will make the public ready to take action.

Burawoy utilizes the radicalism movements of the 1960s as a way to show public sociology's great role in society. He says that in the 1960s, sociological research churned and resulted in increased understanding of racial minority and women stances in the greater society. After this, women and racial minorities seemed to work for greater power in the capitalistic world.

PUBLIC SOCIOLOGY CRITICISM

Many people who practice public sociology do not, exactly, prescribe to the Michael Burawoy described public sociology methods. In the years after Michael Burawoy's election to the presidency of the American Sociological Association, the subject of public sociology has reached a high level of debate amongst sociologists and academic journals.

Many sociologists argue that public sociology overestimates the morality and political agendas of sociologists. They maintain that every single social issue involves moral dilemmas; however, so many of them lack moral clarity. For example, sociologists understand what is morally just; they understand that equality should exist throughout society. However, what they understand "should" happen does not have any bearing in scientific research.

A notable critic of public sociology is sociologist Mathieu Defiem from the University of South Caroline. He said that public sociology is neither sociology nor public. He said that public sociology is not meant to make the scientific study of sociology more presentable to a public audience; it isn't meant to connect to political activity. Defiem states that sociologists must be public intellectuals of the sociological sciences they study. They shouldn't be activists trying to engage a movement.

APPLIED SOCIOLOGY

Applied sociology and academic sociology are quite different. Applied sociology might be more of what Burawoy is working for, while academic sociology is what Defiem is trying to maintain. Essentially, applied sociology is intervention utilizing sociological academia. Therefore, sociologists utilize their understanding in public settings like universities and small communities in order to improve conditions. They solve everyday problems, attempt to improve drug courts, and work for better development for aging populations.

Applied sociology aims to deepen understanding on practical, public issues. These applied sociologists hope to enable research to support their understanding in order to improve community conditions. They seek to utilize sociological efforts to do good deeds on the ground level.

Many universities have begun gearing their curricula toward this applied sociology. Courses lend students the understanding of how to work with clients, with victims, and with people in drug rehabilitation centers. The courses marry the knowledge of sociology with fields like clinical social work and marriage and family therapy.

Chapter 8. Analysis and Social Research

Social research is the general research social scientists conduct in order to better understand society. The research utilizes a systematic plan; however, methods vary and can be quantitative or qualitative.

Quantitative Plans work through social structures with quantifiable evidence. They often create statistical analysis in order to find general claims about a certain subject. These claims must be valid and reliable.

Qualitative Plans work through direct observations of social structures. These plans emphasize subjective accuracy instead of the quantitative plan's generalities.

Most social research methods actually combine quantitative plans with qualitative plans for a more rounded understanding of social structures. For example, most qualitative plans must create structured coding in order to understand the data its undertaken—thus shading into quantitative areas.

Social scientists utilize many methods in order to ensure proper analysis of social structure: census survey data, analysis of single people's social experiences, monitoring street-level crime rates, and investigating old historic papers. These noted statistics formulate the basis of all sociology: from political science to media studies.

SOCIAL RESEARCH METHODS

Different social scientists rely on different research techniques in order to develop their own social theories. Their chosen research methods generally relate back to their historical understanding of the root of sociology. Some acknowledge positivism, for example, while other acknowledge antipositivism more readily. Although quantitative and qualitative approaches are incredibly different, they both require a relationship between theory and data.

A researcher's desired investigation administers how, exactly, that researcher will build a study. For example, if the researcher hopes to find a statistical generalization over the entire community, he might write a questionnaire and send it to that community. On the other hand, if a researcher hopes to have a better, contextual understanding of social actions, that researcher might undertake open-ended interviews or participant observation.

SAMPLING

When researchers hope to understand something general about a population, they cannot work within the realms of the entire world. Therefore, they'll take a "sample" population to provide a more manageable subset of people. Collecting information from these sample groups, in the sociology world, is known as sampling. These sampling methods can be random or non-random. Sampling is often much quicker and much more money-conscious than utilizing a complete census.

Methodological Assumptions in Social Research

All social research is based on both empirical and logical observations. All conducted research is meant to revise or make sense of any theories sociologists might have. It is meant to find patterns in social structures and understand greater social groups; it does not mean to peg down individuals.

Research is divided into two separate fields: pure research and applied research. Applied research actually attempts to alter something in the real world, while pure research holds no ready application.

The process of social research involves an initial creation of a theory. Afterwards, there is operationalization, or the measurement of variables. Next, there are observations, which is the actual collection of the data that one is meaning to collect.

Glenn Firebaugh's Guidelines for Good Research

Sociologist Glenn Firebaugh analyzes the principles for proper research.

1. You should always maintain the possibility for surprise in your social research. Essentially, this means that you mustn't hold a blind spot for what's in front of you just because you thought you would receive a very specific answer.
2. In your research, you should always look for differences that actually make a difference to your study.

3. You should build reality checks into your research design.
4. You should always replicate your design in order to see if an identical research yields a similar result from a different group of subjects.
5. Compare your research with one variable with the same research with another variable.
6. Study the change between your research sessions when you utilize one variable versus another variable.
7. Remember that your method is the means to your desired answer. Therefore, you must fit your research to the research issue—not fit the research issue to your method.

ETHICS OF SOCIAL RESEARCH

When studying people, sociologists must maintain strict ethics in order to respect personal space.

RESPECT PEOPLE.

Researchers must remember that all individuals are "autonomous agents" who can make their own decisions. Any individual without this autonomous agency must be treated with very special understanding.

BENEFICENCE.

The researcher must continually keep the subject of research from harm. Furthermore, the research conducted must bring aid and benefits to greater society. If the research has no tangible benefit to society, it is unethical.

JUSTICE.

The benefits of a particular research session must be distributed appropriately. This fairness is relayed on a case-by-case basis.

Chapter 9. Social Theory

Social theories are developed by sociologists in order to explain or uncover social phenomena. This theory is an initiation between two or more concepts. This theory explains precisely how or why a particular phenomenon formulates in a society.

Look to a social theory example in the work of Robert Putnam. Putnam's work found that American's community involvement in things like clubs, religious participations, or voting has declined over the past fifty or sixty years. Putnam's theory on the reasons for this are vast. However, one of his very prominent reasons is the increased television consumption. The more television people watch, he states, the less they'll want to be involved in their community. This sentence illustrates sociological theory. It proposes an initiation or a relationship between these two concepts: television watching and community involvement. In this case, this relationship is inverse. Therefore, as one increases, the other decreases.

Sociological theory has many levels: grand theories, micro-range theories, middle-range theories, and micro-range theories.

The Importance of Social Theory

Analyze the Robert Putnam theory listed above: that more television watching leads to decreased community involvement. The sentence contains data: the amount of television watched and the amount of community involvement. It further contains a relationship. Data by itself would not be informative because it wouldn't prescribe something very intrinsic about society. Theory allows relationship to take form in order to better understand the surrounding world.

Another Social Theory relationship was formed in Emile Durkheim's Suicide work, discussed in previous chapters. His studies on suicide, a sort of phenomenon, looked at surrounding data in order to try to make a connection between this data and suicide. Through his studies, he was able to connect suicide with religious affiliation. He learned that Protestants were far more likely to commit suicide than Catholics. He further explained that Protestants had weaker social ties, thus pushing them into weaker social cohesion. Therefore, he was able to conclude that Protestants commit suicide more often than Catholics because they are more solitary and lonelier, overall. He was able to make a link between religion's affect on loneliness and suicide.

MAJOR SOCIOLOGICAL THEORIES

There are several broad sociology theories or perspectives that provide great understanding of social life. These theories are used today and cited because of their strength against years of criticism.

None of the below theories are exactly better than any other. Rather, these theories act as complementary pieces in a grater society puzzle.

STRUCTURAL FUNCTIONALISM

An entire chapter in this book is dedicated to Structural Functionalism, a broad theory in sociology. Its original idea was to explain a greater society as an organism with various "organs" pumping away to reach a common livelihood, a common goal. Later on, this theory changed into the ways that social institutions meet greater social needs. The theory is most notably drawn from the workings of Emile Durkheim, who wanted to explain society's ability to be stable and solid over time.

Essentially, society's pieces are bound together, working unconsciously in a quasi-automatic way toward equilibrium. As mentioned in previous chapters, however, structural functionalism is unable to speak of social change. Its focus is, primarily, on social equilibrium.

CONFLICT THEORY

Another entire chapter in this book is dedicated to the social theory of conflict. This is almost a direct aversion to structural functionalism in that it sees society as not an entire unit, working together as one. It sees a dichotomy: two sides in a society scraping for scarce resources. The powerful people will do anything to maintain their power—including downgrading the poor. The poor is left to scrape by with what they can have and sell their ability to work to the higher classes. Unlike Structural Functionalism, however, conflict theory accounts for change as a result of these conflicts. Conflict theory understands that change can occur very suddenly; it can be a kind of revolution.

Limitations of conflict theory align with the fact that society is not constantly changing radically. Conflict theory doesn't account for small or gradual changes.

SYMBOLIC INTERACTIONISM

Symbolic Interactionism theory tries to form a relationship between humans and their greater society. This approach says that humans, the individuals, are responsible for acting instead of allowing their societies to act upon them.

ROLE THEORY

A micro scientific study of society is found in role theory. This role theory relates to the ways in which people "perform" during the day to a sort of audience. These roles are also relationship roles: things like friend, brother, or teacher. Role theory relates the fact that each role as a pre-disposed expectation for the appropriate actions. For example, a teacher's expected role is to teach someone how to read, how to add sums, etc. This expectation would alter the ways in which he acted out his role.

Role theory states that the people who fill certain roles in a society automatically have a significant amount of predictable behavior. For example, if someone is a teacher at school, that same someone might demonstrate teacher-ly actions outside the school. Therefore, one's role in a social structure might play a larger role in one's individual behavior.

Role Theory prescribes to the following ideas:

1. Individuals spend much time participating in larger groups or organizations.
2. Each individual in these groups fills a specific role.
3. Each role maintains a set of functions that the person

with the role must perform.
4. Individuals perform their roles in relation to prior
   norms. Therefore, individuals are conformists who
   just try to live up to what the role requires.

Chapter 10. Focus on Feminism

Feminist theory is one of the greater social theories of the last century. It analyzes men and women's status in the greater society in order to better the lives of women everywhere. Further feminist questions have begun to look at the difference between women of different class, race, age, and ethnicity in order to lend a better, more understanding voice to women. Feminism hopes to allow women to have greater power and to recognize the various ways women have contributed to society.

Four Feminist Theories:

Gender Differences

The gender difference perspective in relation to feminism tries to understand how women's environmental location and experience of that surrounding location differs from men's experiences in that location. For example, feminists try to pinpoint different feminine values that alter the ways in which men and women experience the social world. Other feminists proclaim that the institution, society-run roles given to women and men formulate these gender differences. For example, there's always been an unspoken sexual division of household labor.

Gender Inequality

Gender inequality theories understand that women's experience of social situations is different than men's; they also understand that women's experiences are also unequal.

These theories argue that patriarchy and society have worked against women—women who have the same capacity and agency as men. Therefore, women are isolated in their households without a political voice for years. Furthermore, feminists study the fact that women who are married have higher levels of stress than both men who are married and women who are unmarried due to the unequal assignments of labor at home.

GENDER OPPRESSION

This theory argues that women are not only unequal and different from men in society; it argues that women are actively oppressed and abused by men. Men have the power in most societies, and, as Marx argued, men are prone to keep their power from the women population—either consciously or unconsciously. The theory explains that being a woman is a positive thing; however, societies often do not recognize this and push down upon it, squelching its power.

STRUCTURAL OPPRESSION

Feminists often argue that oppression and inequality of women is a direct result of racism, patriarchy, and capitalism. They agree with Karl Marx's theories about a dichotomy between the few upper class and the great working class. This theory understands that not all women experience the same oppression or the same inequality. It understands that women of different races and ethnicities experience all sorts of different discrimination.

SOCIOLOGY AND YOU

The science of sociology analyzes every aspect of your life: the way you eat, the way you drink, the way you correspond with your friends and co-workers. It works to understand these social structures. From this understanding, these social theories take form: social theories on feminism, functionalism, and conflict theory. Social theories are important to try to bring a common ground to each group of people. They are important to try to bring the lower class better knowledge about why they should be fighting for better living and working conditions. Sociology demands your attention because it proclaims the injustices and unfairness of society in a very scientific and tangible way. Look at the research, look at the findings and make your own assessment. Should you get out into the world and start trying to change the sway of that research? Should you try to help the wealthy class merge with the lower class? Only when you ask yourself these questions can the world rev forward into a better future.

About The Author

The mission of Jonny Bell is to be able to help inspire and change the world, one reader at a time.

This author wants to provide the most amazing life tools that anyone can apply into their lives. It doesn't matter whether you have hit rock bottom in your life or your life is amazing and you want to keep taking it to another level.

If you are like this writer, then you are probably looking to become the best version of yourself. You are likely not to settle for an okay life. You want to live an extraordinary life. Not only to be filled within but also to contribute to society.

He has been studying and applying psychology for over 5 years and met a lot of interesting people along the way. With these writings, Bell wants to keep inspiring others to change for the better.

OTHER BOOKS BY JONNY BELL

Sociology: A Practical Understanding of Why We Do What We Do

Emotional Intelligence: A Practical Guide to Mastering Emotions: Emotions Handbook and Journal

Cognitive Behavioral Therapy: CBT Essentials and Fundamentals: A Practical Guide to CBT and Modern Psychology

Social Psychology: Essentials and Fundamentals: A Practical Guide to Social Psychology and Sociology

Applied Psychology: Practical Guide to the Human Mind, Step-by-Step Advice to the Understandings of Psychology

Sports Psychology: Inside the Athlete's Mind: High Performance - Sports Psychology for Athletes and Coaches

Positive Psychology: Research and Applications of the Science of Happiness and Fulfillment: New Field, New Insights

Spirituality: A Practical Guide to Spiritual Awakening: A Journey of Self-Awareness and Spiritual Growth

POSITIVE PSYCHOLOGY:

Research and Applications of the Science of Happiness and Fulfillment

NEW FIELD, NEW INSIGHTS

JONNY BELL

WHY YOU SHOULD READ THIS BOOK

This book will help you understand a revolutionary branch of psychology: positive psychology. Positive psychology, jolting from the traditional, depressing psychologies of day's past, prescribes the ways in which you can find true, internal satisfaction. It no longer lingers upon what is wrong with you; instead, it pushes you to ask: what is right with me and how can I improve upon that? How can I utilize my talents in order to maximize my life while I'm living it and achieve true self-satisfaction. You can be happy in the face of adversity and stress. You can push beyond lack of confidence, pessimism, and helplessness in order to achieve your goals and reach self-actualization? The book outlines research-driven concepts to allow true happiness to implant itself in your life. It quantifies decades of understanding about what makes humans happy or unhappy, and lands with a firm grasp on: yourself.

Chapter 1. Comprehending Positive Psychology

Positive Psychology: the new psychology revolution swooping through the world, is asking the most interesting question: how can one be happy? Positive Psychology is the inverse of what is traditionally termed "regular" psychology. While regular psychology works to rectify psychological problems, to instill hearty, better mental states after mental trauma, positive psychology works to build positivity and satisfaction in normal life. The swerve from mental instability psychology to positive psychology is relatively recent; the interest in health and mental growth churned to the scene sometime in the past half century after many years of pegging people into mental institutions and studying their brains. Why not study the brain of a health person and try to scientifically administer greater health and happiness upon that person's life? Why not work to discover the ways in which a person can work toward a better, more fulfilling life? These are the general questions behind the exciting new field.

Positive Versus the Negative

Essentially, the "regular" psychology school's focus upon faltering human development doesn't tell the entire story of a person's brain life. Simply knowing what occurs in the brain after stress, after schizophrenia has kicked in, or after emotional trauma has occurred lends the view of a ruptured brain. One can completely understand how a "ruptured brain" works—or ultimately falters on a cellular, minute level. But how can one understand the ruptured brain without paying attention to a full, hearty brain? The full, hearty brain begins with all of its "pieces" in place: that is, it's healthy, full of vibrancy. Nothing is going wrong. However, most brains start out in this normal state. Something: life experience, choice, or environment triggers the brain to ultimately falter or reach to great, happy heights. The topic of positive psychology, then, tries to study the happy, healthy brain in order to help other brains to reach this magnificent, positive balance. Just as traditional psychology works to rectify a faltering brain, positive psychology works to push the brain forward: to ultimate life and joy.

THE OVER-ARCHING GOAL OF POSITIVE PSYCHOLOGY

The ultimate goal of positive psychology on a personal-level is, essentially, to learn the ways in which one can think through the neuron path to joyful emotions. Negative thoughts—on a drastic level—lead to brain disorders and counter-intuitive living. Therefore, positive psychology provides the idea that positive thoughts lead to brain growth and fulfillment. Of course, these positive thoughts—brought on a very person-level—vary from person to person. Not all emotions are the same.

Furthermore, "positive emotions" are not meant to completely eliminate negative emotions. Human beings have immense subtlety; basic positive emotions are swayed and "colored in" by gray, negative emotions. Think of an example: a person achieves great success and graduates from a university. One would think that this person feels the utmost satisfaction at the graduation ceremony: after all, he's worked through many achievements and had to think positively for many years in order to reach this goal. However, for very personal, environmental reasons, his graduation ceremony may be "colored in" by a negative emotion. For example, his father could have died the previous year, therefore missing out on his graduation and lending him feelings of sadness. This does not work against the feeling of joy he feels for graduating; instead, this negative emotion fills out the satisfactory feeling, giving it a complete, human edge. Despite the unhappiness he feels, he still feels immense joy. It's complicated: but what involving humans isn't complex?

THE THREE ISSUES OF POSITIVE PSYCHOLOGY

Positive psychology looks to three main issues during its research and analysis of the human brain and body.

POSITIVE EMOTIONS

Positive emotions study the ways in which a person is happy and content with one's past events, happy in one's present situation, and hopeful for one's future. Therefore, one can feel pleasure from these three sectors. One can remember things that happened in the past and feel joy; alternately, past events can haunt a person, causing unfortunate mental blockings on the road to happiness. One can feel happiness from the hope one feels for the future. This can range from big ideas to small ideas. One can be happy about Christmas around the corner or fueled with the passion to study law in the coming years at a major university. Either of these situations brings hopeful joy. Present joy varies from day to day, obviously, based on current environmental factors. Positive psychology studies the ways in which one's present environment works against or fuels a happy mindset. It studies the ways in which the present brings satisfaction.

POSITIVE INDIVIDUAL TRAITS

Positive individual trait studies in the field of positive psychology lend an understanding of the ways in which a person's talents bring satisfaction and life joy. These talents could be natural: the ability to sing or dance, for example. They could be fueled by one's work environment: the talents one brings to the office in order to write the next big news story or work through the goals of the company. Everyone has inner strengths, inner virtues to push them toward a better, more fulfilling life. Not everyone uses these strengths and virtues wisely. Many are wasted.

POSITIVE INSTITUTIONS

The positive institution methods are based upon the strengths and virtues that stem from various institutions in one's life. These institution-led strengths bring joy and fulfillment to a community of people—providing a unit of safety and inclusion throughout a group. This, essentially, brings a level of relationship joy and satisfaction. It provides something to reflect one's self upon: one can compare one's self to the satisfaction of the community. If the community is fulfilled, provided with institutions that lend fulfilling relationships, one can assimilate into this environment and prosper.

Chapter 2. History of Positive Psychology

Understand the intricate history of positive psychology and the great waves it has created in the past fifteen years.

The Early and Mid Twentieth Century

Prior to the Second World War, psychology worked much like it does today: it worked to cure all mental diseases via mental hospitals and therapists; it worked to provide fulfilling and satisfactory lives for patients; and it worked to identify high talent and further that talent's way into the greater world.

Unfortunately, the years after World War II changed everything. Psychology became primarily cure-based. Therefore, there wasn't a sense to improve something that wasn't already broken. This could have been a result of the war; the nation had been through great traumas, and improving that which had been broken was on the minds of everyone. Abnormal behavior and mental illnesses had to be squashed. Post-traumatic stress disorder (PTSD) hadn't been recognized yet; however, psychologists knew the tragedy of war on the human brain in a very broad sense. They worked to repair it.

Abraham Maslow

During these subsequent "abnormality-focused" years after World War II, a few psychologists chose to focus on humanistic psychology. Abraham Maslow was one of these driving forces, one of the first in the game.

While working alongside Gestalt psychologist Max Wertheimer and Ruth Benedict, an anthropologist at Brooklyn College, Maslow was incredibly alert. He found both Benedict and Wertheimer to be exceptional: highly attuned to themselves, to their happiness, and to their careers. He later took note of their sure happiness and success as he cultivated his humanistic psychology.

Abraham Maslow created theories about self-actualization, peak experiences, and hierarchy of needs.

The hierarchy of needs displays five stages that a man must attain in order to focus on his internal happiness. One must first maintain one's biological health; afterwards, one can find safety, a place to call one's home, relationships, self-esteem fulfillment, and—ultimately—self-actualization.

SELF-ACTUALIZATION: MASLOW'S THEORY

Self-Actualization, one of Maslow's humanistic psychology theories, prescribes the idea that what a man can become, he must become. If he has met the other four stages of the hierarchy of needs and sees his potential laid out before him, he must reach that potential. It is the idea that one can become more full, more complete in one's self.

Self-actualization affects people in incredible ways, according to Maslow's theory. Self-actualized people take joy in solving problems in the greater, external world: problems that don't involve them. They feel a sense of personal responsibility. It allows for a deep sense of appreciation; self-actualized people see the world around them with a sharp eye, every-

understanding that their lives are incredible, that each experience brings a sense of wonder.

Furthermore, self-actualized people reap the rewards of solitude. They enjoy their human relationships, of course; after all, relationships lie on the third step of the hierarchy of needs. However, the self-actualized person needs a few hours to breathe by himself every single day. This way, he can focus on who he wants to be and meeting their full potential.

The self-actualized person further reaches another one of Maslow's theories. He reaches peak experiences. The peak experience is a moment of ecstasy: one cannot fully grasp the intense joy one fells during these experiences. It is a moment of pure bliss. Afterwards, one feels completely rejuvenated and electrified. These peak experiences actually inspire one to further one's life, to reach for greater self-actualization.

Abraham Maslow's work is incredibly important; he pushed the limits of psychology from the 1950's mainstream, abnormal-focused realms. His theories are currently widely accepted with the resurgence of positive psychology.

MARTIN SELIGMAN AND THE RESURGENCE OF POSITIVE PSYCHOLOGY

1998 brought the election of the new president of the American Psychological Association. Martin Seligman stepped up to the position, bringing with him a new psychology theme: positive psychology. He lent all the modern ideas currently utilized and researched today: that the mind can ultimately decide to be joyous and satisfied and happy. In 2009, just eleven years later, the first World

Congress on Positive Psychology took the reigns in Philadelphia, allowing the world to understand the research and the explosion of life-affirming science currently pulsing from the realms of positive psychology. At the convention, Seligman was a featured speaker. These days, he is widely regarded as the ultimate father of positive psychology.

CHAPTER 3. POSITIVE PSYCHOLOGY RESEARCH ANALYSIS

Read more ...

Positive Psychology: Research and Applications of the Science of Happiness and Fulfillment: New Field, New Insights

ONE LAST THING...

If you enjoyed this book or found it useful I'd be very grateful if you'd post a short review on Amazon. Your support really does make a difference and I read all the reviews personally so I can get your feedback and make this book even better.

Thanks again for your support!